My Little Memory Verses

**Illustrations by
Stephanie McFetridge Britt**

Compiled by Brenda C. Ward

WORD PUBLISHING
Dallas•London•Vancouver•Melbourne

My Little Memory Verses

MANAGING EDITOR: Laura Minchew
PROJECT EDITOR: Brenda C. Ward

Library of Congress Cataloging-in-Publication Data:

Bible. English. New Century. Selections. 1994.
   My little memory verses / illustrated by Stephanie
McFetridge Britt; compiled by Brenda C. Ward.
   p.   cm.
   ISBN 0-8499-1140-0
   1. Bible—Quotations. [1. Bible Selections.] I. Britt,
Bs391.2.B375   1994
220.5'208cdc20

94-5480
CIP
AC

Printed in the U.S.A.

4 5 6 7 8 9 LBM 9 8 7 6 5 4 3 2 1

*Your word is like a lamp for my feet
and a light for my way.*

PSALM 119:105

CONTENTS

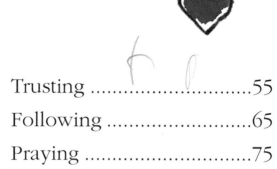

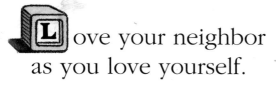ove your neighbor
as you love yourself.

LEVITICUS 19:18

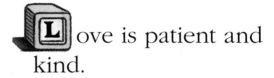ove is patient and kind.

1 CORINTHIANS 13:4

Be kind and loving to each other. Forgive each other just as God forgave you in Christ.

EPHESIANS 4:32

If someone does wrong to you, do not pay him back by doing wrong to him.

ROMANS 12:17

Do for other people
what you want them to
do for you.

LUKE 6:31

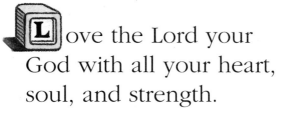ove the Lord your God with all your heart, soul, and strength.

DEUTERONOMY 6:5

We know that in everything God works for the good of those who love him.

ROMANS 8:28

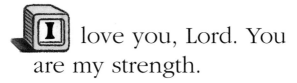 love you, Lord. You
are my strength.

PSALM 18:1

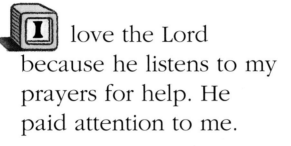 love the Lord
because he listens to my
prayers for help. He
paid attention to me.

PSALM 116:1-2

For God loved the
world so much that he
gave his only Son. God
gave his Son so that
whoever believes in him
may not be lost, but
have eternal life.

JOHN 3:16

Yes, I am sure that nothing can separate us from the love God has for us.

ROMANS 8:38

Christ's love is greater than any person can ever know. But I pray that you will be able to know that love.

EPHESIANS 3:19

Surely your goodness and love will be with me all my life.

And I will live in the house of the Lord forever.

PSALM 23:6

As high as the sky is above the earth, so great is his love for those who respect him.

Be full of joy in the Lord always. I will say again, be full of joy.

PHILIPPIANS 4:4

Give thanks to the God of heaven. His love continues forever.

PSALM 136:26

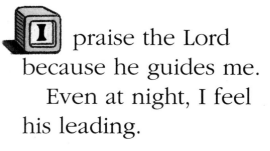 praise the Lord because he guides me. Even at night, I feel his leading.

PSALM 16:7

It is good to praise the Lord, to sing praises to God Most High.

PSALM 92:1

Depend on the Lord. Trust him, and he will take care of you.

PSALM 37:5

Give all your worries
to him, because he cares
for you.

1 Peter 5:7

But the people who trust the Lord will become strong again.

They will be able to rise up as an eagle in the sky.

They will run without needing rest.

They will walk without becoming tired.

ISAIAH 40:31

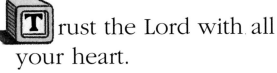rust the Lord with all your heart.

Don't depend on your own understanding.

PROVERBS 3:5

Do not forget to do good to others. And share with them what you have.

HEBREWS 13:16

Remember the Lord in everything you do.
And he will give you success.

PROVERBS 3:6

Children, obey your parents the way the Lord wants. This is the right thing to do.

EPHESIANS 6:1

My God, I want to do
what you want.
 Your teachings are in
my heart.

Psalm 40:8

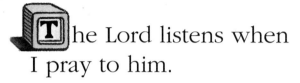The Lord listens when I pray to him.

PSALM 4:3

Always be happy.
Never stop praying. Give
thanks whatever
happens.

1 THESSALONIANS 5:16–18

Do not worry about anything. But pray and ask God for everything you need.

PHILIPPIANS 4:6

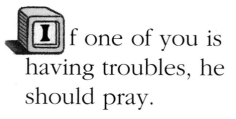 f one of you is having troubles, he should pray.

JAMES 5:13

Each one should give, then, what he has decided in his heart to give. He should not give if it makes him sad. And he should not give if he thinks he is forced to give. God loves the person who gives happily.

2 CORINTHIANS 9:7

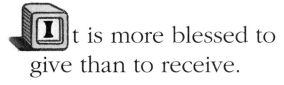It is more blessed to give than to receive.

ACTS 20:35

Honor the Lord by giving him part of your wealth.

PROVERBS 3:9

Give, and you will receive. . . . The way you give to others is the way God will give to you.

LUKE 6:38